Cambridge Primary
English
Second Edition
Workbook 1

Sarah Snashall

Series editors:
Christine Chen
Lindsay Pickton

Boost

HODDER
EDUCATION
AN HACHETTE UK COMPANY

Registered Cambridge International Schools benefit from high-quality programmes, assessments and a wide range of support so that teachers can effectively deliver Cambridge Primary. Visit www.cambridgeinternational.org/primary to find out more.

Third-party websites, publications and resources referred to in this publication have not been endorsed by Cambridge Assessment International Education.

Acknowledgements
The Publishers would like to thank the following for permission to reproduce copyright material. Every effort has been made to trace or contact all copyright holders, but if any have been inadvertently overlooked, the Publishers will be pleased to make the necessary arrangements at the first opportunity.

Text acknowledgements
p. 23 © 'Kookaburra Sits In The Old Gum Tree' Words & Music by Marion Sinclair © Copyright 1934 and Renewed 1989. Happy as Larry Music Publishing Pty Ltd. 4/30-32 Carrington St, Sydney NSW 2000 Australia. All Rights Reserved. International Copyright Secured. Lyrics reproduced by Permission of Hal Leonard Europe Limited and adapted with Permission of Chester Music Limited trading as Campbell Connelly & Co; **pp. 52–53** text/illustrations from *NOT SO FAST, SONGOLOLO* by Niki Daly. Copyright © 1985 by Niki Daly. Reprinted with the permission of Margaret K. McElderry Books, an imprint of Simon & Schuster Children's Publishing Division. All rights reserved; **pp. 30–32** *Year Full of Stories*, written by Angela McAllister and illustrated by Christopher Corr*, published by Frances Lincoln Children's Books, an imprint of The Quarto Group, copyright © 2016. Reproduced by permission of Quarto Publishing Plc.; **p. 56** © Tom Percival, 2018, *Ruby's Worry*, Bloomsbury Publishing Plc.; **p. 62** 'Rumble in the Jungle' by Giles Andreae from *Rumble in the Jungle* by Giles Andreae. Text copyright © 1998 Giles Andreae. Reproduced with kind permission of Coolabi Group Limited.

* Illustrations on pages 30–32 are not by Christopher Corr.

Photo acknowledgements
p. 12 *tl, cr*, p. 19 *tl, cr*, p. 26 *tl, cr*, p. 36 *tl, cr*, p. 43 *tl, cr*, p. 50 *tl, cr*, p. 60 *tl, cr*, p. 66 *tl, cr*, p. 72 *tl, cr* © Stocker Team/Adobe Stock Photo; **p. 13** *br* © Fayee/Adobe Stock Photo; **p. 48** *b* © P Studio/Adobe Stock Photo; **p. 67** *tr* © Alek Sorel/Adobe Stock Photo.

t = top, *b* = bottom, *l* = left, *r* = right, *c* = centre

Orders: please contact Hachette UK Distribution, Hely Hutchinson Centre, Milton Road, Didcot, Oxfordshire, OX11 7HH. Telephone: +44 (0)1235 827827. Email education@hachette.co.uk. Lines are open from 9 a.m. to 5 p.m., Monday to Saturday, with a 24-hour message answering service. You can also order through our website: www.hoddereducation.com

© Sarah Snashall 2021

First published in 2021 by
Hodder Education
An Hachette UK Company
Carmelite House
50 Victoria Embankment
London EC4Y 0DZ

www.hoddereducation.com

Impression number   10 9 8 7 6 5 4 3 2 1
Year   2025 2024 2023 2022 2021

Cover illustration by Lisa Hunt

Illustrations by Steve Evans and Vian Oelofsen

Typeset in FS Albert 17/19 by IO Publishing CC

Printed in the United Kingdom

A catalogue record for this title is available from the British Library.

9781398300217

Contents

Note to teachers: This Workbook should be used alongside the *Cambridge Primary English Learner's Book 1*. Learners should complete the activities in the Learner's Book theme first. For complete coverage of the Cambridge Primary English Stage 1 curriculum framework, the Workbook cannot be used in isolation and must be used alongside the Learner's Book. The *Self-check* chart at the end of each unit in this Workbook refers to objectives covered in both the Learner's Book and Workbook units. Support for the Learner's Book and Workbook (including activity answers) can be found in the *Cambridge Primary English Teacher's Guide 1*.

Aqsa's Adventures

1 Finish the words.

Say the word first and listen to the sounds you need. Write the sounds.

a
t r ____ ____

b
c ____ ____ ____

c
h ____ ____

d
s ____ ____ ____

2 Tick (✔) the book that is a fantasy story. Tell a partner why.

3 Complete the sentences using these words: *fell, monster, hat*.

a Aqsa _____ into the washing machine.

b The _____ was purple and furry.

c The _____ was red .

4 Read these words. Circle the words with the **oa** spelling pattern.

boat

pop

hat

goat

hop

bag

toad

loaf

road

hoop

say

5 Circle the correct spelling.

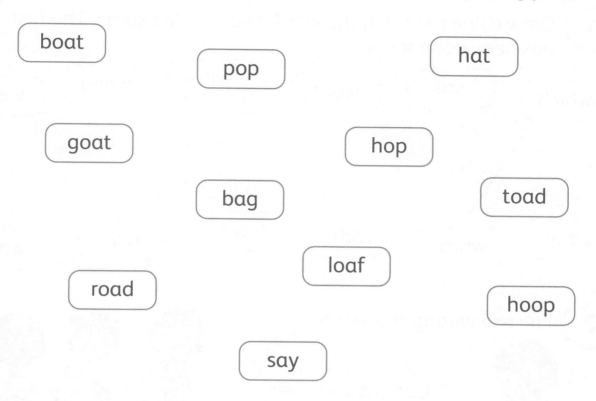

a

queen

quen

b

lef

leaf

c

teeth

teth

d

peas

pes

Strange places – familiar words

1 Draw a line to match the words that are the same. The first one has been done for you.

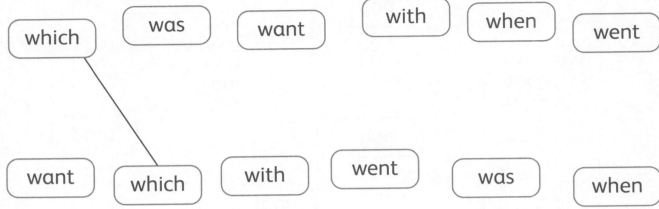

| which | was | want | with | when | went |

| want | which | with | went | was | when |

2 Practise writing the words.

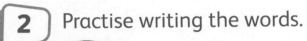

Use Look – Cover – Write – Check.

Read	Write	Read	Write
most		called	
trees		of	
look		off	
asked		monster	
my		which	
said		was	

Sentences

 1 Circle the capital letter and full stop in each sentence.

a I want cake for supper.

b The hat has a bobble.

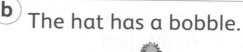

c We go into the cave.

d She walked by the river.

2 Use the words to write a sentence. Remember to use a capital letter and a full stop.

a tree was a by Aqsa

_____

b clouds two saw sky in the I

_____

c pointed a seashell Aqsa at

_____

d she cloud in a jumped

_____

3 Can you add the three full stops missing from these sentences?

Aqsa looked for the plopper cropper She looked up and down She found it by the river

Aqsa

 1 Draw a line to match each feeling to a picture.

frightened

happy

surprised

 2 Use the words below to complete the sentences.

Think about how each person is feeling.

fluffy | washing machine | yellow | apple pie | jingling

a Dad looks nice in his _____ shirt.

b Ava likes to wear her _____ top.

c I can hear the _____ of the keys in the door.

d Put your clothes in the _____.

e Sim ate _____ for dinner.

Words, words, words

 Read the words.
Sound out each word.

 Use the pictures to help.

bedroom

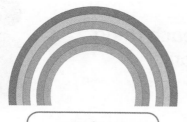

rainbow

tree

road

 Where did the mother plopper cropper chase Aqsa next? On a separate sheet of paper, write a sentence for each picture. Use these words:

bedroom   rainbow   tree   road

along   around   up   over

Write your sentences like this:

a
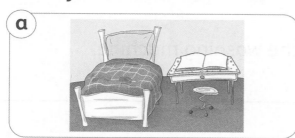
She chased Aqsa <u>around</u> the <u>bedroom</u>.

b
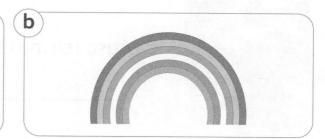
She chased Aqsa _____ the _____.

c

She chased Aqsa _____ the _____.

d
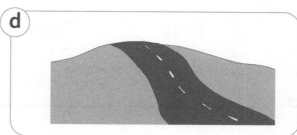
She chased Aqsa _____ the _____.

Beginning, middle and end

 Write beginning , middle or end next to each part of the story.

Think about when each thing happened in the story.

a Aqsa chased the plopper cropper.

_____

b Aqsa woke up.

_____

c Aqsa fell into the washing machine.

_____

 Write a word to show when these things happened.

First   Then   At last

a _____, Asqa fell into the washing machine.

b _____, Asqa chased the plopper cropper.

c _____, Aqsa woke up.

My fantasy story

1 Use the words to complete the chart.

| birds | glasses | bowls | dishes |

| buses | monsters | boxes | eggs |

Ends in **s**		Ends in **es**	

2 Choose and copy the correct word.

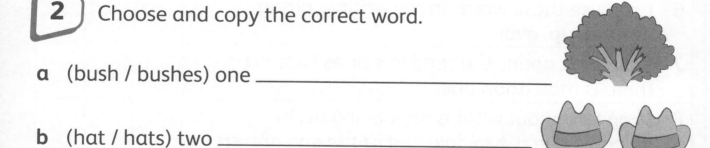

a (bush / bushes) one _____

b (hat / hats) two _____

c (sock / socks) two _____

d (box / boxes) three _____

e (bird / birds) one _____

Self-check

 I can do this.

 I can do this, but I need to keep trying.

 I can't do this yet.

What can I do?			
1 I can hold my pencil correctly.			
2 I can say what a fantasy story is.			
3 I can use a capital letter and a full stop in my sentences.			
4 I can tell a friend who the main characters are in a story.			
5 I can blend sounds to try and read new words.			
6 I can use these words in my writing: **along**, **around**, **up**, **over**.			
7 I can spot nouns that end in **s** or **es** to show there is more than one.			
8 I can talk about what is happening at the beginning, in the middle and at the end of a story.			
9 I can plan and write a new story with a beginning, a middle and an end.			
10 I can tell a friend a story I know.			

What do you need more help with? Write the number or numbers.

I need more help with:

_____

_____

Unit 2 Non-fiction: Recount texts

Postcards

1 Read the postcard aloud.

> Dear Ravi
>
> Hello from Dubai.
> We have come to
> visit Auntie Jazmine.
> Today, I saw the
> tallest building in the
> world. The top was
> in the clouds.
>
> Love Diya

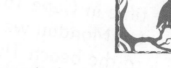

Ravi Lal

4321 Sunny Street

Chennai

Tamil Nadu 600078

India

2 Use coloured pencils. Circle a word that has:

- a capital letter for the start of the sentence in red.

- a capital letter for **I** in green.

- a capital letter for a person's name in blue.

- a capital letter for the name of a place in yellow.

3 On a separate sheet of paper, copy these sentences and correct the capital letters.

a i visited dubai.

b yesterday, i had an ice cream.

Read this postcard aloud. Add the missing full stops.

Dear Diya

We have had a fun
time in Cape Town
On Monday we went
to the beach Then
we went to the forest
Yesterday we had a
picnic in the forest

Love Ravi

SOUTH AFRICA

5 Write Diya a postcard from Cape Town. Use this postcard or a
separate sheet of paper.

Check that you have used capital letters for names
and sentences.

Dear Diary

1 Complete each sentence. Add a full stop at the end!
Use these words: ⟨ funny ⟩ ⟨ jumped ⟩ ⟨ boring ⟩

a My uncle was loud and _____

b We played and _____ in the pool

c The trip was hot and _____

2 Write the words in these sentences in the correct order.

a my cousin to Benji. I went see

_____

b me the eggs. showed Benji

_____

c the eggs cooked for lunch. We

_____

3 Match the beginning and end of the sentences. Draw a line.
The first one has been done for you.

I like juice	and red.
I have a sister	and Mum likes coffee.
My cousin plays tennis	and a brother.
Our car is old	and football.
Granny tells stories	and sings songs.

A trip to the zoo

 1 Read this recount text about a trip to the zoo aloud. Circle the nouns that end in **es**.

A noun is a person, place or thing.

Last Thursday, Mr Sinna, who is a zookeeper, visited our school. He showed us the brushes and mops he uses to keep the zoo clean. Mr Sinna had two boxes of food with him. He showed us the food for each animal and some of the dishes he uses. There were a lot of carrots and bunches of bananas! He showed us pictures of monkeys hanging from branches and foxes hiding in bushes.

 2 Write the words under the correct heading in the table.

Remember, the verb shows what the noun is doing. Verbs sometimes end in **ing**.

crocodiles snapping

bees buzzing

birds hopping

 spiders spinning

monkeys chatting

Noun	Verb
snakes	sliding

My first day of school

 1 Circle the verbs that show the action happened in the past.

> Verbs with **ed** show that the event has already happened.

a We go / went to school.

b I was / am scared on my first day at school.

c We work / worked all day.

d We walked / walk from home to school.

e Sim helped / helps us to find our classroom.

f Min showed / shows us where to put our shoes.

g I had / have lunch at school.

2 Use these words to complete the sentences.

(At last)   (First)   (Next)   (Then)

a _____, I packed my school bag.

b _____, I walked to school with Mum.

c _____, we waited in the playground.

d _____, we went into the classroom.

Growing up

1 Add the ending to the verb. The first one has been done for you.

	Add **s**	Add **ing**	Add **ed**
walk	walk**s**	walk**ing**	walk**ed**
play			
cook			
jump			
look			
ask			
pick			
call			

2 Read the sentences. Circle the verb with the correct ending.

a I started / starting school last year.

b Yesterday, Dad pulled / pulling out my tooth.

c Look, the baby is crawling / crawled!

d I have been grows / growing taller.

e I like cooked / cooking with Gran.

f I can walk / walked home on my own now.

Self-check

 I can do this.

 I can do this, but I need to keep trying.

 I can't do this yet.

What can I do?			
1 I can say what a recount is.			
2 I can say what sort of words I might find in a recount.			
3 I can find time words in a recount.			
4 I can use capital letters for people, places and **I**.			
5 I can use **and** to add more information to a sentence.			
6 I can spot nouns and verbs in sentences.			
7 I can read verbs with different endings.			
8 I can tell a friend about something that happened to me.			

What do you need more help with? Write the number or numbers.

I need more help with:

_____

_____

Counting in the Caribbean

 1 Practise writing the number names.

Look at the word. Say the word. Cover the word. Write the word. Check it!

	1st go	2nd go
one		
two		
three		
four		
five		
six		
seven		
eight		
nine		
ten		

2 Read the words on each line. Find the words that rhyme.
a Cross out the word that does not rhyme.
b Circle the words with the same spelling pattern.
The first one has been done for you.

one	sun	none	home
two	new	how	few
three	tree	them	sea
four	fork	pour	saw
five	hive	fine	I've
six	sticks	socks	mix
seven	Kevin	sender	eleven
eight	bright	weight	wait
nine	fine	night	sign

An English alphabet

1 Say each letter name. Trace over the letters. Then write the letter on the line underneath.

a   b   c   d   e

f   g   h   i   j

k   l   m   n   o

p   q   r   s   t

u   v   w   x   y   z

An animal rhyme from Australia

1 Read this rhyme from Australia. Can you learn it off by heart?

Kookaburra sits in the old gum tree,

Merry merry king of the bush is he,

Laugh Kookaburra, laugh Kookaburra,

Great your life must be!

2 Circle the words that rhyme.

| be | Merry | tree |

| king | he | is |

3 Find and copy a word in the rhyme with these spelling patterns:

sh _____

gr _____

st _____

tr _____

A lullaby from China

1 Read these words aloud. Find out the meaning of any words you do not know.

glowing   silver   bright   shooting   diamond   dark

velvet   twinkling   shining   climbing   sleeping

watching   swooping   calling

2 Use the words to complete this poem. Choose one or two words for each line. Then write three more lines using your own ideas.

Use this frame or a separate sheet of paper.

_____ night

_____ stars

_____ moon

_____ owl

_____ child

_____

_____

_____

A kite rhyme from Japan

 Read the sentences. Underline all the nouns.
Circle all the verbs.

> A noun is an object, place or thing. A verb is a 'doing' word. Think about what the noun is doing!

a The kite zooms up in the sky.

b The wind plays with the kite.

c The kite dances up and down.

d The children hold on tight.

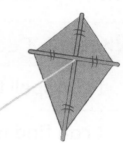

2 These sentences are missing capital letters and full stops.
Write them correctly on a separate sheet of paper.

a yesterday Riku and i went to the park

b we took our kites out of the bag

c i held the kite and riku held the string

d we ran and the wind took the kite high

e we took turns to hold the string

Unit 3 Poetry: Traditional rhymes

Self-check

 I can do this.

 I can do this, but I need to keep trying.

 I can't do this yet.

What can I do?			
1 I can spell the number names from one to ten.			
2 I can find words that rhyme.			
3 I can form my letters in the correct way.			
4 I can say the alphabet from **a** to **z**.			
5 I can use interesting words in my poems.			
6 I can find a noun in a rhyme.			
7 I can find a verb in a rhyme.			
8 I can use capital letters to start a sentence and for names.			

What do you need more help with? Write the number or numbers.

I need more help with:

_____

_____

The ungrateful tiger

1 Look at the main characters from the story *The ungrateful tiger*. Answer each question.

a What is Tiger like?

_____

_____

b How does Tiger feel?

_____

_____

c What is the man like?

_____

_____

d How does the man feel?

_____

_____

2 Use your own ideas to complete each sentence. Use **and** to say two things in each sentence.

a   I am _____ and _____.

b   The weather today is _____ and

_____.

c   Tigers are _____ and _____.

d   I like _____ and _____.

3 On a separate sheet of paper, use the word **and** to join these sentences. The first one has been done for you.

a   The man hears Tiger. The man helps Tiger.

   The man hears Tiger **and** helps him.

b   Tiger is hungry. Tiger is cross.

c   The story is about a tiger. The story is about a man.

d   Rabbit sees the man. Rabbit wants to help.

e   The jungle is hot. The jungle is hilly.

f   Tiger slips. Tiger falls in a ditch.

The trick

 Ask an adult to read this traditional tale. Point and listen.

Once upon a time, there was a big and proud lion. All the animals were frightened of him, except for a little brave mouse. He liked to show off to his friends by running up and down the lion's back when he slept. But one day – thwack – the lion caught the little fellow.

'Don't eat me,' cried the mouse.

'Why not?' asked the lion.

'Because I might save your life one day!'

The lion thought this was so funny that he let the little mouse go.

But it so happened that the very next day, the lion was caught by some hunters. They tied the lion up in thick rope.

The lion growled and moaned but he could not escape. He had been lying there for a day when the mouse found him. At once he started to nibble at the ropes until at last the lion was free.

'Thank you, friend,' said the lion.

'You see,' said the mouse, 'small can be strong too.'

a What is the mouse like? Join two words with **and**.

The mouse is _____.

b What is the lion like? Join two words with **and**.

The lion is _____.

 Complete the sentence. Use your own words.

This story is about _____

_____.

Tiddalik the Thirsty Frog

 1 Draw a line to match the picture to the feeling.

uninterested
happy
cross
sad

 2 How do these characters feel? Write the word.

a baby kangaroo _____

b Tiddalik _____

c wombat _____

3 What do the characters do in the story? Draw a line to match the animal to the words.

told a joke
drank the water
said they should make Tiddalik laugh
asked for the water

4 Write a joke for Kookaburra to tell Tiddalik. Read your joke to a friend.

Tiddalik shares

1 Are these sentences correct? Make a tick (✔) or a cross (✘).

A sentence must have a verb. The words in a sentence must be in the right order.

	Correct	Not correct
Tiddalik slurped up the water.	✔	
Wombat about the water.		✘
Wombat shouted at Tiddalik.		
Tiddalik at Platypus laughed.		
The water everywhere.		
Tiddalik shared the water at last.		
Kangaroo thumped his tail on the ground.		

2 Write all the verbs from question 1 that show the action happened in the past.

Verbs that end in **ed** show the action happened in the past.

_____

_____

3 Correct these sentences. Write the words in the correct order.

a Kangaroo up woke Platypus.

_____

b The water out gushed.

_____

c The water the drank animals.

_____

d were The animals happy.

_____

The King of the Forest

1 Use the pictures to retell the end of the story *The King of the Forest* by writing a caption underneath each picture.

Let me tell you a story

 1 Use the words below or your own ideas to finish the sentences to tell a story.

there was a		in a dark forest		in a dry desert

fox	frog	tiger	sat	hunted

fell	arrived	felt	slept

a Once upon a time, _____.

b Long ago, in Dreamtime, _____.

c Long, long ago, _____.

d There once was, _____.

e One day, _____.

 2 Draw lines to match the sentences with their endings. Read the sentences aloud.

Quick as a flash, the cat	got bored.
In the blink of an eye, the water	reached the top.
All at once, the animals	pounced on the mouse.
After a little while, the boys	ran away.
Before long, we	flooded the land.

Write it down

 1 Choose the correct word from this list to complete each sentence.

(gushed)   (pounced)   (roared)   (boxed)   (danced)

a The tiger _____.

b The lion _____.

c The kangaroo _____.

d The water _____.

e The lizard _____.

Unit 4   Fiction: Traditional tales

Self-check

 I can do this.

 I can do this, but I need to keep trying.

 I can't do this yet.

What can I do?			
1 I can talk about the character in a story.			
2 I can use **and** to join ideas together.			
3 I can talk about the setting of a story.			
4 I can check that each sentence has a verb.			
5 I can find and use verbs ending in **ed**.			
6 I can use some phrases to add detail to my story.			
7 I can collect interesting words from the stories I read.			
8 I can talk about what happens at the beginning, in the middle and at the end of a story.			
9 I can use some story openers to start a story.			

What do you need more help with? Write the number or numbers.

I need more help with:

_____

_____

Do this! Do that!

1 Circle the bossy verb in each sentence.

> Remember, a bossy verb orders you to do something!

a Pick up your toothbrush.

b Put toothpaste on the toothbrush.

c Clean your teeth using a circle movement.

d Spit out the toothpaste.

e Rinse the sink.

2 Choose a bossy verb to complete each sentence in these instructions.

Eat   Sprinkle

Squeeze   Put   Get

a _____ a cone.

b _____ on a scoop of ice cream.

c _____ on sweet sauce.

d _____ on crunchy toppings.

e _____ the ice-cream cone!

Following instructions in order

 Add the missing time words to complete the instructions. Choose from these words:

Finally   Next

First   Then

How to cross the road

1 _____, find a safe place to cross away from parked cars.

2 _____, stand near, but not on, the kerb.

3 _____, look both ways to check for traffic.

4 _____, cross quickly when you see there is no traffic coming.

 Look at the map. Complete these instructions to get to the pool from the park. Add **left** or **right** in each blank space.

right   left

How to get to the pool from the park

1 Come out of the park.

2 Go _____.

3 At the crossroads, go _____.

4 The pool is along the road on the _____-hand side.

Nouns and bossy verbs

1 Write a bossy word for each action. The first one has been done for you.

a _____crawl_____   b _____   c _____

2 Circle all the instructions in this picture. Look for bossy words!

Make a present

 1 Ask an adult to read these instructions. Circle the bossy verbs. Underline the nouns.

How to make a picture frame

You will need:
- 8 craft sticks
- pretty buttons or beads
- a photograph
- a piece of card larger than your photograph
- paint
- glue

What to do:

1 First, paint your craft sticks.

2 Next, stick your photograph to the middle of the piece of card.

3 Wait for everything to dry for a few minutes.

4 Glue two sticks to the top and two sticks to the bottom of the picture card.

5 Glue two sticks to each side.

6 Decorate the frame with beads or buttons.

7 Finally, add a second piece of card to the back to help it stand up.

2 Match each picture to an instruction in question 1. Write the instruction number in the box.

More instructions

1 Write **a** or **an** before each word.

a _____ apple

b _____ party

c _____ present

d _____ invitation

e _____ sweet

f _____ egg

2 Write **a** or **an** to complete each sentence. Underline the bossy verb.

a Pass me _____ apple.

b Find me _____ tin.

c Cut up _____ orange.

d Read _____ book.

e Mash _____ banana.

f Pick up _____ umbrella.

3 Complete the sentences using these words:

| egg | fork | apple | drink |

a Would you like an _____?

b Give me a _____ please.

c Pass me an _____ please.

d I would like a _____ with my snack.

41

4 Words that end in **ly** tell us **how** to do things. Write the missing words. Use these words:

Neatly | Slowly | Quickly | Carefully

You will need:
- a piping bag
- 300 g icing sugar
- 85 g butter
- 30 ml milk
- food colouring
- a piping nozzle

How to decorate your cakes

1 _____ mix together the icing sugar and butter.

2 _____ add the milk and food colouring.

3 Pop the nozzle in the piping bag.

4 _____ put the butter icing into the piping bag.

5 _____ squeeze the icing onto the cakes.

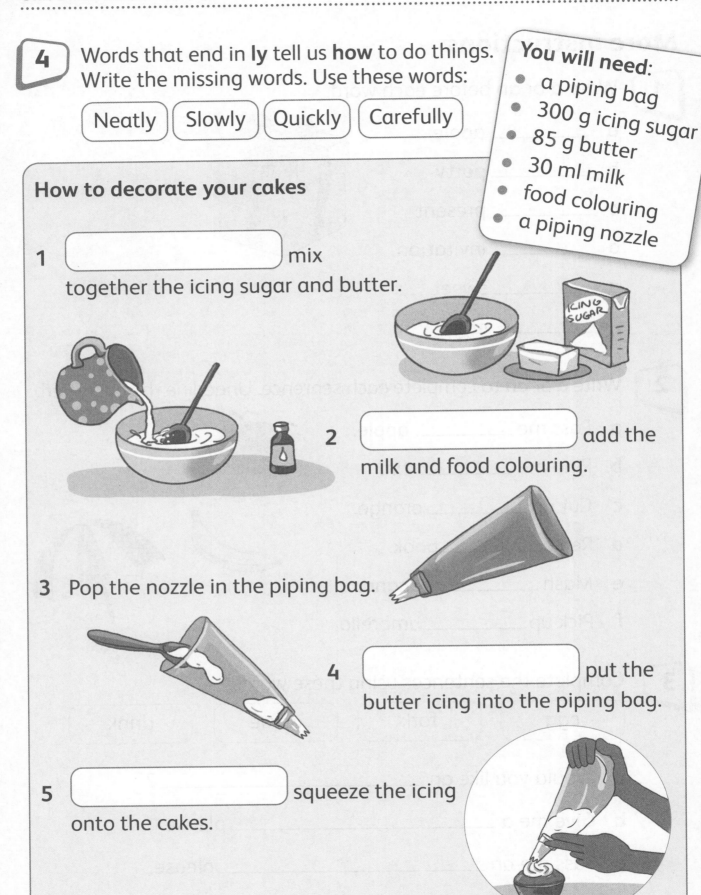

Self-check

 I can do this.

 I can do this, but I need to keep trying.

 I can't do this yet.

What can I do?			
1 I can find the bossy verbs in an instruction.			
2 I can follow instructions step by step.			
3 I can give clear instructions to a friend.			
4 I can use **a** or **an** correctly.			
5 I can use time words or numbers when writing instructions.			

What do you need more help with? Write the number or numbers.

I need more help with:

_____

_____

A rainy day

1 Practise writing the letters with joins.

sh

ch

th

ng

nk

2 Read the poem. Choose your favourite line from the poem. Write it in joined-up writing.

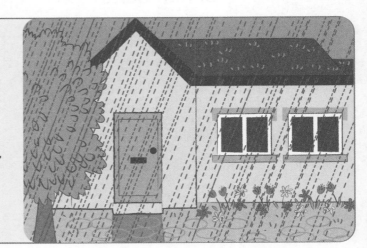

Rain on the green grass,

And rain on the tree,

And rain on the house-tops.

But not upon me!

3 Look at the rainy scene below.

Write two words that go together in each box. The two words can rhyme or sound good together. Use these words.

drip   burbles   drop   huddles   puddles

bubbles   splish   splash

Lightning crashes

1 Write a storm poem inside the lightning flash.
   a Choose a noun to go with the verbs in the clouds.
   b Can you make some lines rhyme?

Hot, hot, hot

1 Draw lines to link the words that rhyme.

| hot | trees | sun | roasting |

| cool | stay | toasting |

| play | bees | spot | pool |

| best | | rest |

| fun |

2 Use the rhyming words that you have found to complete this poem about being hot. Use this frame or a separate sheet of paper.

It is hot in the sun

_____

I'll go in the pool

_____

Let it snow

1 Read these snowy words:

snow   cold   fun   wet

footprints   snowballs

hot chocolate   snowman

hat   sledge   coat   cat

sledging   zoom   sliding

slipping   padding   buried

2 Use some of the words to complete this poem.

Padding means walking along making a soft, dull sound.

Building _____

Flying _____

Padding _____

Drinking _____

It's raining hearts

1 Circle the verbs that end with **ing**.

a   It is the first day of the holidays.

b   We are going to the park.

c   Milly and Josh are coming too.

d   Mum is bringing a picnic.

e   I am wearing my boots in case it starts raining.

f   I am climbing to the top of the slide.

g   Stop pushing, Josh.

h   It is starting to rain.

2 Circle the correct verb in each sentence.

a   Yesterday, it raining / rained chocolate sauce.

b   Tomorrow, it will be pouring / poured pies.

c   I hope it will be snowing / snowed sugar tomorrow.

d   Yesterday, we jumping / jumped in all the custard puddles.

e   Stop shouting / shouted about sweets!

f   I have filling / filled my cup with soda.

g   Look! The jelly baby is crawling / crawled!

Self-check

 I can do this.

 I can do this, but I need to keep trying.

 I can't do this yet.

What can I do?			
1 I can find words that rhyme in a poem.			
2 I can find words with similar sounds in a poem.			
3 I can join some letters when writing.			
4 I can work out how someone feels in a poem.			
5 I can see that some words that rhyme have similar spelling patterns.			
6 I can choose **a** or **an** correctly.			
7 I can be a good listener.			
8 I can find and read verbs ending in **ing**, **s** and **ed**.			

What do you need more help with? Write the number or numbers.

I need more help with:

_____

_____

At home

1 Draw lines to match the pictures to their story settings.

home
school
pirate ship
castle

 2 Look at this character:
- Imagine she arrives in each picture above.
- On a separate sheet of paper, write some sentences to show what happens next.

At the shops

 Who do these shoes belong to? Shepherd   Gogo

Read the story on pages 123–124 in the Learner's Book for a clue!

_____

_____   _____

 How does Shepherd feel at the end of the story? Write some sentences.

_____

_____

_____

_____

_____

_____

3 Gogo and Shepherd go shopping. Can you write some sentences to say what happened? Use these words to help you.

first   then   next   at   last   finally

bananas   socks   drink   stop   shoe   and

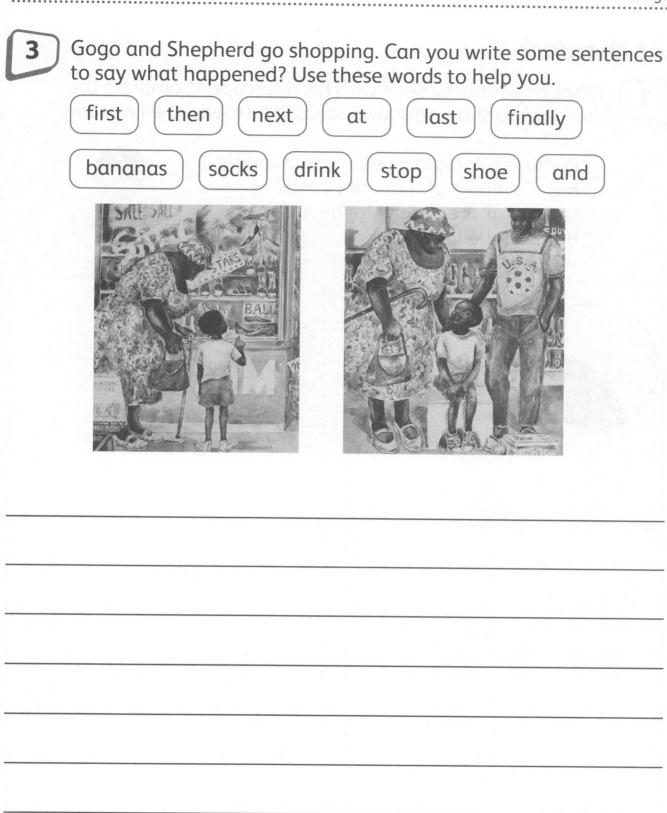

_____

_____

_____

_____

_____

_____

_____

_____

At the park

 What has Timothy seen with his telescope? Complete the drawings to show your own ideas. Write what he has seen.

Perhaps it is a pirate hat or someone's hair. Is it part of a bouncy castle or the top of the slide? Maybe it is a boat on the lake.

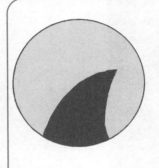

Going on an outing

 1 Rewrite each sentence to add the missing capital letters and full stops.

a uncle arjun jumped in the boat

_____

b cousin padam rocked the boat

_____

c auntie sia sang loudly

_____

d granny parnika laughed with granny nidhi

_____

2 Look at this picnic. Add numbers to show 'how many' and the correct **s** or **es** ending. The first one has been done for you.

a _____two_____ box _es___

b _____ mug_____

c _____ dish_____

d _____ bottle_____

e _____ bush_____

f _____ bag_____

At school

 How does Ruby feel in each picture? Write some sentences.

_____

_____

_____

_____

_____

_____

_____

_____

 What happens to Ruby's Worry? Use these words: **First**, **Then** and **At last**. Write a sentence for each one.

First, _____

_____.

Then, _____

_____.

At last, _____

_____.

Back at the park

 1 Can you remember these words from the story *Ruby's Worry*?

(shrink) (barely) (tumbled) (hovering)

Can you use these words in new sentences?

a The pens _____ out of the bag.

b The balloon was _____ in the sky.

c It was _____ raining so we went out.

d We watched the snowman _____ in the sun.

2 Can you complete this story with these story words?

(All of a sudden) (Once upon a time) (One day) (Then)

You should tell an adult if you feel worried.

_____, there was a boy called

Jack. He was always happy.

_____, had a Worry.

The Worry got bigger and bigger.

_____ he met a girl in the park.

He told her about the Worry. _____

the Worry was gone!

At home again

 1 Read these verbs. Match the verbs to the feelings. Write them in the correct box.

You can put verbs in more than one box.

| grinned | sobbed | shook | cried |

| whispered | laughed |

sad

_____

_____

scared

_____

_____

happy

_____

_____

2 Use two verbs from question 1 to complete each sentence. Use **and** to join the two verbs. The first one has been done for you.

a Bob was sad. He cried **and** sobbed.

b Paulo was scared. He _____.

c Lottie was happy. She _____.

3 Ask an adult to read this text. Can you find all the words starting with the spelling pattern **str**? Write them in the box below.

The island of Struay is very small. It only has one straight street. The street stretches down the island to Granny's house. Katie Morag will stroll along talking to her friends. A ferry brings people from the mainland. In bad weather, the ferry struggles to travel and people are stranded on the island. It is very quiet on the island. If you feel stressed, then come to the island of Struay for a rest. Soon the strangers on the island will be friends.

Self-check

 I can do this.

 I can do this, but I need to keep trying.

 I can't do this yet.

What can I do?			
1 I can say where a story is set.			
2 I can say how a character feels.			
3 I can ask questions about a story.			
4 I can use a beginning, middle and end to plan a story.			
5 I can add **s** or **es** to a noun.			
6 I can read verbs ending in **ing**, **ed** or **s**.			
7 I can look at someone when they are talking.			
8 I can use interesting words when I write.			
9 I can use **and** to make a sentence longer.			

What do you need more help with? Write the number or numbers.

I need more help with:

_____

_____

Bengal Tiger

1 Read the animal names.

a   Point to three pairs of animal names that rhyme.

b   Write three animal names with four syllables.

_____

_____

c   Write three animal names with three syllables.

_____

_____

More animals

 1 Ask an adult to read this poem about jungle animals.

Rumble in the Jungle

There's a rumble in the jungle,
There's a whisper in the trees,
The animals are waking up
And rustling in the leaves.

The hippo's at the waterhole
The leopard's in his lair,
The chimpanzees are chattering
And swinging everywhere.

Some animals are frightening,
And some are sweet and kind,
So let's go to the jungle now
And see who we can find …

By Giles Andreae

a Circle pairs of words that rhyme. Look at the spelling.

b Find and copy two words that start with the spelling pattern **sw**.

_____

c Find these words. Are they quiet verbs or noisy verbs?
Tick (✔) the correct one.

rustling quiet ☐ noisy ☐

whispering quiet ☐ noisy ☐

2 Read the poem again aloud. Can you make it sound interesting to listen to?

Snap, Snap!

1 Read these interesting words from two crocodile poems.
Circle your three favourite words.

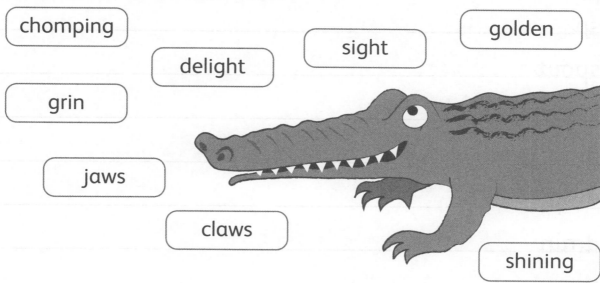

chomping

delight

sight

golden

grin

jaws

claws

shining

2 Use the words from question 1 to write a sentence describing
the crocodile.

_____

_____

3 Use the words from question 1 to write your own poem about
the crocodile. You could start:

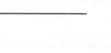

I see the golden crocodile
With its horrible grin
And its terrible jaws …

_____

_____

_____

Incy Wincy Spider

1 Practise joining these spelling patterns and then write the words.

sp

spout

spider

dr

drop

drain

thr

thread

through

cl

climb

cr

crawl

ll

wall

ai

rain

again

My animal poem

 1 Add other animal words you know to these boxes.

If you don't know how to spell a word, use phonics and have a go!

Animal names

armadillo   ox   crocodile

_____

_____

Animal actions

leg by leg   chomping   grins

_____

_____

How animals look

hairy   red   golden

_____

_____

Noises animals make

quack   roar

_____

_____

2 Use your words to write a poem about animals. Write one line for each animal. Use this frame or a separate sheet of paper. You could start your poem like this:

The golden crocodile chomps and grins.
The shaggy ox stamps and puffs.

_____.

_____.

_____.

_____.

_____.

_____.

Unit 8   Poetry: Poems on similar themes

Self-check

 I can do this.

 I can do this, but I need to keep trying.

 I can't do this yet.

What can I do?			
1 I can clap the syllables in a word.			
2 I can talk about a poem I have read and say which poems I like.			
3 I can find verbs, nouns and adjectives in poems.			
4 I can use my voice in different ways to make a poem sound interesting when I read it aloud.			
5 I can collect interesting words in a *Spelling log*.			
6 I can write neatly so that my work looks attractive.			
7 I can write neatly so that my words are easy to read.			
8 I can point out words that rhyme with the same spelling pattern.			

What do you need more help with? Write the number or numbers.

I need more help with:

_____

_____

Reduce, reuse, recycle

1 These words are important in this unit.
Match each word to its meaning.

| Reuse |

| To break down or melt rubbish so that it can be turned into something else |

| Recycling |

| To buy fewer things so that we have less rubbish to throw away |

| Reduce |

| To use a bottle or a bag again instead of buying a new one |

2 Join the labels to the features of this information book.

| main heading | | picture |

| subheading |

Plastic everywhere
There are tiny pieces of plastic in every part of the ocean.
Microplastics
When plastic rubbish breaks apart, it turns into very tiny pieces of plastic. Some of
| main text |
these pieces are too small to see.
Eating plastics
These tiny pieces of plastic are eaten by sea creatures.

Plastic breaks down into tiny pieces.

| subheading | | caption |

Information books

1 Look at the book cover. Read the blurb. Write a title for the book.

Want to reuse
a plastic bottle?
Here are
20 fantastic
craft ideas.

2 Look at the book cover. Write the blurb.

RACING
CARS

Helpful headings

1 Write the missing headings for this text. Choose from these headings:

| Craft projects | Refill bottle | Reusing bottles |

(Main heading) [_____]

There are many ways we can reuse a bottle before throwing it away.

(Subheading) [_____]

If you buy a plastic bottle, refill it with water when it is empty and keep using it.

(Subheading) [_____]

Plastic bottles can be used in many craft projects. They can be made into bird feeders, pencil cases, plant pots and many more things.

2 This pencil case is made from a reused plastic bottle.

Draw something else you could make from a reused plastic bottle.

Write a caption for your picture.

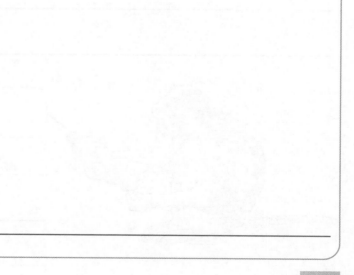

Pictures and diagrams

Write a label for each piece of rubbish. Write why it is dangerous on the lines underneath.

A label doesn't need to be a sentence – it can just be one or two words.

My mini-book

1 Practise joining these letters and words.

ow

flow

ew

flew

igh

flight

ea

sea

oa

foam

ar

star

er

cleaner

bb

rubbish

rr

lorry

Self-check

 I can do this.

 I can do this, but I need to keep trying.

 I can't do this yet.

What can I do?			
1 I can find headings and subheadings in an information book.			
2 I can find the blurb and say what it is used for.			
3 I can point out the title of an information book.			
4 I can find the contents page and use it to find information.			
5 I can write a caption for a picture.			
6 I can find and read a label on a diagram.			
7 I can join up some of my words.			

What do you need more help with? Write the number or numbers.

I need more help with:

_____

_____